Smelling and Tasting

Claire Llewellyn

W

FRANKLIN WATTS
LONDON•SYDNEY

First published in 2004 by Franklin Watts
96 Leonard Street, London EC2A 4XD

Franklin Watts Australia
45-51 Huntley Street
Alexandria, NSW 2015

Text copyright © Claire Llewellyn 2004
Design and concept © Franklin Watts 2004

Series advisers: Gill Matthews, non-fiction literacy
*   consultant and Inset trainer*
Editor: Rachel Cooke
Series design: Peter Scoulding
Designer: James Marks
Photography: Ray Moller unless otherwise credited
Acknowledgements: Chris George/Corbis: 21.Bryan Gibb/Art Directors/Trip: 7b.
Robin Redfern/Ecoscene: 19tr. Jochen Tack/Still Pictures: 18br.
Thanks to our models, including Vanessa Dang, Sophie Hall, Latifah Harris, Thomas Howe,
Amelia Menicou, Spencer Mulchay and Ishar Sehgal.

A CIP catalogue record for this book is available from the British Library.

ISBN: 0 7496 5726 X

Printed in Malaysia

Contents

Smell and taste

Every day we smell and taste things in the world around us. Smelling and tasting are two of our senses.

▶ *We smell things with our nose.*

We have five senses. They are seeing, hearing, tasting, smelling and touching.

We taste things with our tongue.

5

Into the nose

Our nose takes in smells from the air. Smells float through the air.

▶ *We take in air when we breathe. We take in smells, too.*

Nostrils

6

The nearer we are to something, the better we can smell it.

We all have a nose on our face. Find a mirror and look at your nose. What shape is it? Can you see inside your nostrils?

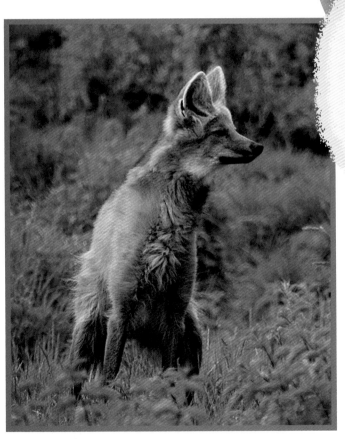

This fox is sniffing the air to pick up smells.

Smells good!

Our noses take in many
different smells.
We like some
smells.

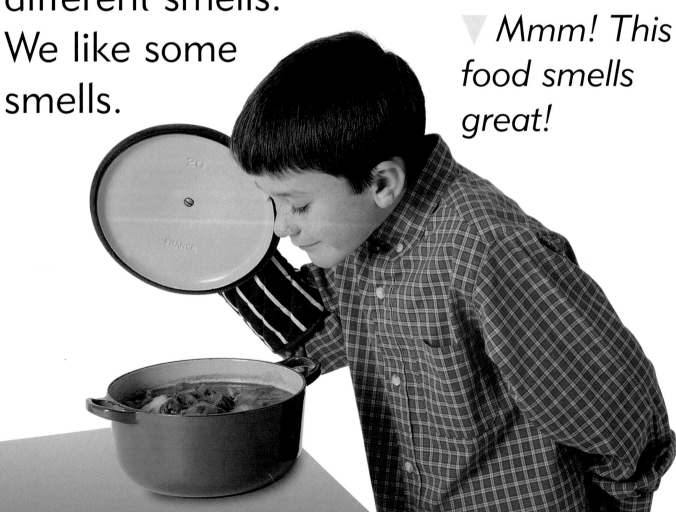

▼ *Mmm! This
food smells
great!*

8

These clothes smell fresh.

These roses smell sweet.

What smells do you like? Make a list of your five favourite smells.

Smells bad!

Sometimes our noses pick up nasty smells. We do not like these at all!

▶ *Ugh! These socks smell dirty.*

▼ *Pooh! The baby's nappy needs changing.*

What smells don't you like? Make a list of the five smells you hate the most.

▼ *Yuck! This egg is bad.*

On the tongue

We taste our food
when we put it
on our tongue.
We move the food
around our mouth
to taste it better.

▶ *Different areas
of our tongue
pick up four
different tastes.*

Tastes bitter

Tastes sour

Tastes salty

When we chew, our teeth break up our food and make it taste stronger.

Tastes sweet

13

Working together

If food smells good, it will taste good, too! We need our sense of smell to taste our food.

▶ *If you hold your nose when you are eating, you cannot taste your food.*

Hold your nose and close your eyes. Ask a friend to pass you pieces of carrot and cucumber. Can you taste which is which?

When we try a new food, we smell it first...

When we have a bad cold and our nose is blocked, we can't smell things well. What happens to our sense of taste?

then we taste a little.

How does it taste?

We don't all like the same tastes. We enjoy different kinds of food.

▶ *A good meal is made up of lots of different tastes.*

Some people love peanut butter.

Everyone has a favourite food. What's yours?

Some people hate it!

17

Keeping safe

Smells and tastes can protect us. They can warn us of danger.

▶ *The smell of smoke warns us of fire.*

▼ *We can smell when food is burning.*

A smell of gas warns us of danger.

A vole sniffs the air as it feeds. It is smelling for hunters or other kinds of danger.

This milk tastes sour. It is not good to drink.

Take care of your body. Don't sniff or taste anything with a strong, nasty smell.

A world of tastes and smells

Our senses of taste and smell help to make life better. They help us to enjoy the world.

 Without our senses, we could not taste lollipops...

20

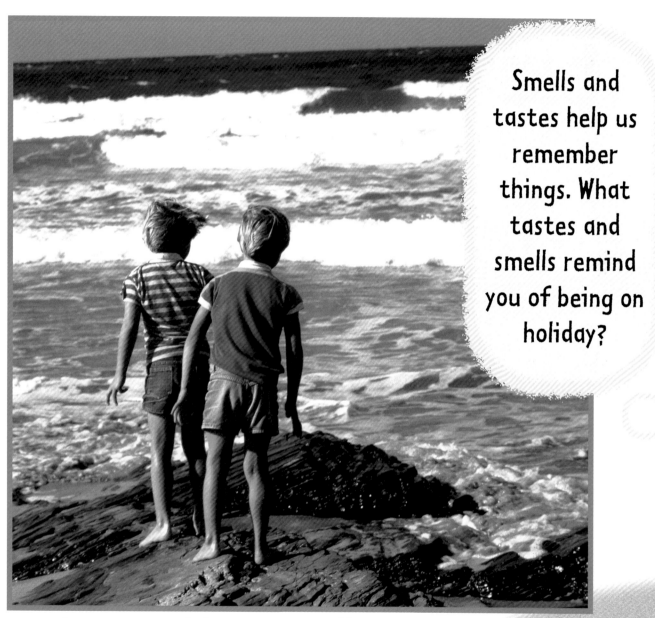

Smells and tastes help us remember things. What tastes and smells remind you of being on holiday?

and we could not smell the sea.

I know that...

1 We smell things with our nose.

2 We taste things with our tongue.

3 Smelling and tasting are two of our body's senses.

4 Our nose picks up many different smells – some good, some bad.

5 Our tongue picks up sweet, sour, salty and bitter tastes.

6 We need to smell our food to taste it.

7 We enjoy different tastes.

8 Smelling and tasting help to protect us.

9 They help us to enjoy the world.

Index

About this book

I Know That! is designed to introduce children to the process of gathering information and using reference books, one of the key skills needed to begin more formal learning at school. For this reason, each book's structure reflects the information books children will use later in their learning career – with key information in the main text and additional facts and ideas in the captions. The panels give an opportunity for further activities, ideas or discussions. The contents page and index are helpful reference guides.

The language is carefully chosen to be accessible to children just beginning to read. Illustrations support the text but also give information in their own right; active consideration and discussion of images is another key referencing skill. The main aim of the series is to build confidence – showing children how much they already know and giving them the ability to gather new information for themselves. With this in mind, the *I know that...* section at the end of the book is a simple way for children to revisit what they already know as well as what they have learnt from reading the book.